Mr Macaroni and the Exploding Pizza Pie

A Play for Children

John Gardiner and Fiz Coleman

A SAMUEL FRENCH ACTING EDITION

SAMUEL FRENCH

FOUNDED 1830

SAMUELFRENCH-LONDON.CO.UK
SAMUELFRENCH.COM

FOR AMATEUR PRODUCTION ENQUIRIES

UNITED   KINGDOM   AND   WORLD
EXCLUDING   NORTH   AMERICA
plays@SamuelFrench-London.co.uk
020 7255 4302/01

Each title is subject to availability from Samuel French,

depending upon country of performance.

CHARACTERS

Mr Luigi Macaroni, owner of "The Pizza Pie Palace"
Wordsworth, a cheeky waiter
Old Nellie, a withered waitress
Drippy Dora, a daft waitress
Eileen Nostril, owner of "Eileen Nostril's Hairdressing Salon"
Norman Nostril, her nephew
Brigadier Bumbracket ⎤
Miss Lolita Suspender ⎬ Mr Macaroni's posh clients
Major Shareholder
Madame Dubonnet ⎦
Captain Kung Fu, an oriental piratical captain
Wun Wong Eye ⎤
Wun Wong Arm ⎮
Wun Wong Leg ⎬ Wing-Wang pirates
Wun Wong Foot ⎮
Wun Numb Bum ⎦
Waiters

Note: The roles of Mr Macaroni's clients, the Wing-Wang pirates and the Waiters who serve at the beginning and between the acts may be tripled-up.

ACT I
Outside Mr Macaroni's restaurant and Eileen Nostril's Hairdressing Salon. They are both situated by the seaside

ACT II
Down by the harbour, on board Captain Kung Fu's useless boat, in the sea and finally back home safely

PRODUCTION NOTES

The Set

The set should be very simple and colourful. The central playing area is a sunlit patio in front of two large entrances. One leads into "LUIGI MACARONI'S PIZZA PIE PALACE" while the other leads into "EILEEN NOSTRIL'S HAIRDRESSING SALON". Although you cannot see into the interiors of these establishments, both exteriors have boldly coloured fronts, names and fittings.

The cyclorama represents a blue sky and c there is a white patio table with a pretty umbrella shade and two white chairs.

The lighting should be warm (pink and straw) and only darken during the mysterious "snake sequence" and the terrifying entrance of the Wing-Wang pirates.

There should be two posters on the set advertising "FATIMA PHIL-POT—FAMOUS FORTUNE TELLER—ON THE PIER DAILY". There should also be similar posters in the auditorium.

Scenery may be struck at the end of Act I or flown, but if this is inconvenient the first half of Act II can be lit and played downstage, while the rear half of the playing area may be darkened. When Dora, Nellie and Wordsworth return safely home the lights may then simply come up to reveal the two entrances again. This simple manoeuvre in no way spoils the effectiveness of the play.

A gangplank should be set permanently. It should project from the front of the stage right into the audience. The Chinese junk can be assembled and struck quickly and efficiently during the exploding of the pizza pie.

The sound of seagulls at times throughout the play will give the desired seaside mood. A piano may be used to accompany the songs and make appropriate sound effect noises wherever required.

The Presentation

The play may be performed as it stands but if a company wishes to add more fun and zest to the participation, the auditorium could be set out as an extension to the restaurant on stage. The audience would be seated at the tables with the programmes doubling as menus, the only course on sale being pizza which can be served with a wide range of revolting relishes (see sample Menu/Programme).

The pizza orders should be taken as the audience arrive, the company taking the roles of Waiters. Certainly Nellie, Wordsworth and Dora should stand out early on. They should be incredibly noisy, shouting out orders at the tops of their voices, making a great kerfuffle and generally getting in the way of everyone and everything.

The pizzas ordered are served during the interval. They can be free or charged for, depending on finances. Some children do not like pizza and it is wise to have Italian ice-cream and drinks available as an alternative. Mr Macaroni should be stationed at the main entrance to the auditorium to welcome the audience. He makes a tremendous fuss of all his guests, gets their names and announces them. He directs waiters to take them to their numbered table.

Waiters polish the chairs, flick fluff off the tablecloths and dust down the children. Mr Macaroni clips the ears of any waiters who step out of line. Stepping out of line would involve cleaning out the ears of children or checking their necks for tidemarks etc.

Tablecloths can be cheap paper ones. Bottles with candles help to make a cosy atmosphere. Tickets should be sold by table letter and number, e.g. Table A Seat 1.

Costumes
A few guidelines for your help in dressing the play.
Macaroni Full morning-suit. Immaculate. Carnation in button-hole. Hair slicked down, parted in the middle. Curly Italian moustache. Sideboards.
Wordsworth A walking wreck. Everything too large from black baggy trousers to a huge white shirt and filthy waistcoat. He has a big bow tie and big boots.
Nellie She should look like Old Mother Riley. Black skirt, white Victorian blouse and old woollen cardigan with holes at the elbow. Hairnet. Floppy slippers.
Dora Although dopey, Dora should be lovable and attractive. Bright skirt and sweater (bright yellow/orange/pinks). Hair tied in two bunches with big colourful bows. Pencils clipped to sweater or pocket. Bright coloured tights or long socks. One tooth blacked out.
Waiters Big black baggy trousers. Brightly coloured bow ties cut out of washing powder cartons ("Daz", "Dreft" etc.). White shirts, pencil moustaches. Women as well as men should be dressed in this style. Like silent movie waiters.
Eileen Tight pencil skirt in black satin. Frilly green or turquoise blouse. Whatever colour you choose it should be vulgar and utterly tasteless. Blue rinse wig. Heavy make-up. High-heel shoes. In Act II the wedding dress should be really lovely and Eileen's make-up and approach to clothes have taken a turn for the better.
Kung Fu Eighteenth-century coat, cravat, white blouse. Dead parrot on shoulder. Crutch. Kung Fu headband with symbols. Chinese make-up. He should be right over the top.
Wing Wangs Tights. Three-quarter length Chinese dressing-gowns with Chinese symbols, or Judo jackets. Kung Fu headbands. Sashes. Each should have a physical disability in keeping with his name, e.g. Wun Wong Arm has a hook. Chinese make-up.
Lolita Smart dress, full-length fur coat, dark glasses, bubble blonde wig.

Bumbracket   Topi, khaki shorts, khaki jungle jacket, khaki socks, boots and monocle.

Shareholder   Dark suit. Fur-collared overcoat. Top hat, cane.

Dubonnet   Twenties shimmering Charleston dress. Ostrich feather head-dress. Beads, paste bracelet, cigarette holder. Could be accompanied by non-speaking Toulouse-Lautrec on knees.

MENU

PIZZA PIE SPECIAL

~~~

PIZZA SPECIAL PIE

~~~

SPECIAL PIZZA PIE

All Main Courses above are
absolutely free of charge & served
with a side-salad of ~ old rubbish,
dirty vegetables, unwashed 'things',
and filthy fag-ends

Thank you. Please call again.

P.S. I love Eileeno Nostril

signed
Marcello Macaroni
X

ACT I

A patio in front of two large entrances. The entrance R *leads into "LUIGI MACARONI'S PIZZA PIE PALACE" and the entrance* L *into "EILEEN NOSTRIL'S HAIRDRESSING SALON". There is a white patio table with a pretty umbrella and two white chairs* C. *To one side, there is a menu slate. There are posters on stage (and also in the auditorium) advertising "FATIMA PHILPOT—FAMOUS FORTUNE TELLER—ON THE PIER DAILY". A gangplank projects from the front of the stage into the audience*

Mr Macaroni and his Waiters welcome the audience as they arrive. When Mr Macaroni is satisfied that the audience are settled in, he jumps on the stage and blows a whistle for silence. One Waiter continues making a noise and he has to blow again

Macaroni Welcome everyone to the Pizza Pie Palace of——
All —Luigi Macaroni!

The Lights come up suddenly. The House Lights fade and the Waiters come on stage

Macaroni That'sa me. And my pizza pies are——
All —supremo! Superbo!
Wordsworth Pafetick!
Macaroni "Pafetick!" What do you meana pathetic? What can be better than Luigi Macaroni's pizza pies.
Wordsworth (*after a pause*) Fish 'n' chips!
All Yeah! I love fish 'n' chips! Much better! Cor, delicious mate!
Macaroni Fish and chips? Chish and fipperies? (*He thinks*) You're right. Tomorrow we sell pizza pies and the fish and chipperies.
All Hooray. (*They sing and dance*)

SONG 1 (*Tune: Funiculi, Funicula*)

Pizza pie and lovely fish'n'chips
Eat some pizza, thena lick your lips
A pizza pie
A fish'n'chips
A pizza pie
A fish'n'chips
Lovely pizza pies and
Delicious fish'n'chips.

Macaroni OK. Stoppa da muckin' about.

All Stoppa da muckin' about.
Macaroni Clean uppa da kitchen.
All Clean uppa da kitchen. (*They start to exit*)
Macaroni While I go and count uppa da lovely money.
All (*stopping dead in their tracks*) Da lovely money?
Macaroni Exactimunto. Last week I only makea da fifty quid.
All Fifty quid! Cor!
Macaroni Si. And it'sa not enough. That'sa why some of you will be getting the old canvas bag.
Dora What's that mean?
Nellie The sack, stupid.
Dora Oh yeah.
Wordsworth Blimey.
Macaroni Yes, some of you will be feeling the old booterooji. You three —(*indicating Wordsworth, Nellie and Dora*)—one, two, fifteen—line up there. The rest, scram!

Wordsworth, Nellie and Dora line up as requested

The other Waiters exit

Now you (*to Dora*), what'sa your name?
Dora D-D-Dora, Mr Tapioca, sir. Drippy Dora.
Macaroni Macaroni is my name. What do you mean, "Drippy" Dora?
Nellie She does daft fings, sir.
Dora Yesterday I went window shoppin' wiv me mum.
Macaroni And?
Dora I come back wiv five windows.

They laugh suddenly and stop suddenly

Wordsworth She's a loony, sir.
Macaroni And what is your name?
Wordsworth Wordsworth, sir.
Macaroni What kind of a name is thata?
Wordsworth Me dad likes daffodils, sir.
Nellie And I'm old Nellie.
Macaroni You're Nellie, Nellie.
Wordsworth With the big fat——
Macaroni What!?
Wordsworth —kneecaps, sir. She's got very big kneecaps.
Dora She's a greengage fancier.
Macaroni Greengage fancier?
Nellie Old age pensioner, daft head!
Dora Oh yeah.

Macaroni strides away as the other three shunt across stage to a new position

Macaroni OK. You three thinka yourself pretty smarta dickory docks eh? Well from now on I shall be keeping an eye on all of you.
Wordsworth Ay. Ay.

Macaroni And after I've counted uppa the day'sa takings I shall give you a test of efficiency.

Dora Is that like sums?

Macaroni It's exactly likea da sums.

Dora I ain't no good at them.

Macaroni Good. Then I shall have mucha pleasure in giving you the old booterooji! (*Quietly*) Ha!

All (*copying him*) Ha!

Macaroni Ha ha ha!

All Ha ha ha!

Macaroni Hee hee, ha ha . . . *etc.*

Macaroni exits cackling

The others mimic him

Nellie 'Ere stop all that nonsense—this is serious. We're for the push.

Wordsworth The boot!

Dora The canvas bag!

Nellie Right, Drippy.

Wordsworth We'd better convince old Macaroni that he really needs us to run the Pizza Palace.

Nellie I can't afford to lose my job.

Dora I couldn't get another job. Nobody wants drippies. (*She breaks away* L)

Wordsworth Ah never mind, Dora. We'll fink of somefink.

He opens his arms to enfold her but deliberately misses her, and Dora walks into the pros arch

Nellie (*signifying the kids in the audience*) 'Ere I wonder if the young 'uns would 'elp us?

Dora Oh yeah.

Wordsworth Good finkin', Nellie. (*To the audience*) If we could work out some way of getting Macaroni to keep us on, would you give us a hand?

The audience responds

All (*ad lib*) Yeah—thanks very much—that's great.

Nellie Right.

Dora Right.

Nellie OK.

Dora OK.

Wordsworth What?

Dora What?

Wordsworth What we gonna do?

Dora Oh yeah.

Nellie Well, I'm good at adding up. If we could prove to him that I'm a Wonder Granny—(*she does a little spin like "Wonder Woman"*)—at maths, he might let me keep the accounts.

Dora I ain't no good at sums.

Wordsworth What's four plus four?

Dora Seventy-two.

Wordsworth (*to the audience*) That's not bad, is it?

Nellie Not bad? That's useless. I can count up anything.

Wordsworth All right big-head. How many fingers and thumbs have you got?

Nellie Eleven!

Wordsworth (*laughing*) Pafetick. Everyone knows you've only got ten fingers and thumbs.

Nellie That's 'cos you're daft, Wordsworth. Look. (*She counts backwards on her left hand*) Ten—nine—eight—seven—six—(*holding up her right hand*)—and five's eleven.

Wordsworth Blimey!

Dora That's magic, Nellie. 'Ow d'yer do it?

Nellie Wonder-Granny brain-power. I eat up all me greens.

Wordsworth 'Ere. Old Macaroni loves all that magic stuff.

Dora We could use a trick to fool him.

Wordsworth⎫
Nellie   ⎬(*together*) We could use a trick to fool him.

Wordsworth We could do some "maths magic" to amaze Macaroni. When 'e comes back we'll ask him to write down any number he likes on the menu slate over there, while you've got your back turned, Nellie.

Nellie So I can't see what he's written?

Wordsworth That's it. Then you tell him what number 'e's written.

Dora Magic! But 'ow will she know, Wordsworth, she can't see the number.

Wordsworth That's where the trick comes in.

Dora Does it?

Wordsworth Certainly. We'll ask one of our mates out there (*signifying the audience*) to write Macaroni's number down on a piece of your paper, Dora, and hold it up for Granny Nellie to see.

Nellie Grannytastic! (*To the audience*) Would you do that?

Ad libbing, they pick a child from the audience to help them later. Dora gives the child a piece of paper and a pencil

All Thanks very much. (*They sit at the table* c)

Dora These people are nice, ain't they?

Wordsworth Course they are.

Dora They don't shout at yer like Mr Macaroni.

Wordsworth No.

Nellie What we gonna do about Dora keeping her job, Wordsworth?

Wordsworth Yeah. That is a problem.

Nellie Wotcher good at, Dora?

Dora Nuffin'.

Wordsworth That's a great start.

Dora 'Ere's my last school report. (*She produces her school report from up her knicker leg and hands it to Wordsworth*)

Wordsworth (*reading it*) "English—flippin' useless. French—très bonkers. Science—please find enclosed a bill for one science lab."

Nellie You must be good at somefink, Dora.

Dora I don't fink so, Nellie.

Wordsworth 'Old on.

All 'Old on.

Wordsworth We'll give her a general knowledge test like they do on *Mastermind*.

Nellie (*importantly*) So we can assess her IQ.

Wordsworth Exactly, my old Nellie baby. Ready, Dora?

Dora Yes. (*She sits in a chair*)

Quiz-game music starts to play as the Lights fade down to a spot on Dora

Wordsworth Nellie, the questions.

Nellie hands him a question paper

Your name is?

Dora Pass. No, I mean . . . Drippy Dora. 'Ere it's gone all dark.

Wordsworth Your occupation?

Dora Useless waitress . . . part-time.

Wordsworth Your special subject?

Dora Daft Fings.

Wordsworth Right, Drippy Dora, here are your questions on Daft Fings. How do you stop dogs digging up the garden?

Dora Hide all the shovels.

Wordsworth Correct. What do hedgehogs eat on Sundays?

Dora Prickled onions.

Wordsworth Correct. What are furry, crunchy and squeak when you pour milk over them.

Dora Mice Crispies.

Wordsworth Correct. And finally how do you start a flea race?

Dora One, two, flea go.

Wordsworth Correct. Drippy Dora, you have scored on your special subject——

Dora That's it!

The Lights come up

Nellie That's what?

Dora That's what I can do.

Nellie What's that what you can do?

Dora I can show Mr Macaroni how I can bump off all the fleas and bluebottles that come in his restaurant.

Nellie You mean flit 'em.

Dora Yeah, stop 'em buzzin' the burgers and pooin' on the pizzas.

Nellie How do you do that, Dora? ·

Dora By using my diabolical dirty dishcloth. (*She pulls a filthy rag, which has things like "FILTH", "MUCK", "BOGEYS" etc. written clearly on it, from her knicker leg*)

Nellie
Wordsworth } (*together*) Poo! What a filthy diabolical pong!

Dora That kills all known germs stone deaf.

Wordsworth Great idea, Dora and the kids can help us with the sound effects. Right, if we all make bluebottle buzzin' sounds, Macaroni will think he's been invaded by nasties.

Nellie He'll pull his hair out!

Dora He hates bluebottles.

Wordsworth Then we'll show 'im how important Dora's diabolical dirty dishcloth is.

Nellie (*to the audience*) Yeah, you could all scream and pretend to die like bluebottles when you see Dora's cloth.

Wordsworth Let's have a practice.

The audience all buzz and on a signal Dora whips out her dishcloth and they all scream and die

No, that's not loud enough. Macaroni will think you've only been wounded—you gotta give really 'orrible screams as if you're being squelched and squelched.

Nellie Let's try again.

There is a satisfactory repeat of diabolical horror

Dora That was much better, Wordsworth.

Nellie Look out, here comes Macaroni.

Marcaroni enters

Macaroni OK. Sit down over there you three.

They sit at the table

All Yes, Mr Macaroni.

Macaroni And donta fidget.

All (*grinning*) No, Mr Macaroni.

Macaroni And donta grin.

All Three bags full, Mr Macaroni.

Macaroni (*parading*) Right. My ristorante is overstaffed. It'sa too small so three people gotta get the old booterooji. Then with the extra money I can expand.

Wordsworth Don't sack us, Mr Macaroni—we're more useful to you than you think.

Macaroni Really?

All Really!

Macaroni Righta. You—(*to Nellie*)—whata can you do?

Nellie I'm magic at maths, Mr Macaroni. I could keep an eye on all your financial accounts.

Macaroni Accounts?

Nellie Yeah. Fiddle the figures.

All Fiddle the figures.

Nellie Juggle the budget.

All Juggle the budget.

Nellie I can even tell what numbers people are thinkin' of, without seein' 'em.

Macaroni Impossible.

Wordsworth No it's not, Mr Macaroni. You write down a number on the menu slate over there (*pointing*) and Nellie will be able to tell you what you have written without lookin'. Turn your back, Nellie.

Macaroni This is ridiculous. Any number, you say?

Dora Any number you like.

Macaroni Okey dokey.

Nellie turns her back on Macaroni to face the audience. Macaroni writes a number on the slate and at the same time the child in the audience writes the number on the paper for Nellie to read

Dora Happy with that, Mr Macaroni?

Macaroni It's a good number.

Dora He says it's a good number, Wordsworth.

Wordsworth Now Nellie, without looking at the slate can you tell us what number Mr Macaroni has written down?

Nellie Using my superhuman Granny powers I think the number is—— (*She gives the number that Macaroni has written*)

Macaroni (*aghast*) Incredible. But I'm sure that this is only some silly conjuring trick. You will leave by the end of the week.

Nellie Oh no!

Macaroni Oh yes. (*He cackles*)

Wordsworth Poor old Nellie. (*He comforts her*)

Macaroni (*to Dora*) You are next—Drippy Doughnut isn't it?

Dora Drippy Dora, sir.

Macaroni That's whata I said. Now what can you do?

Dora I can help you with your tight jeans.

Macaroni Tight jeans?

Wordsworth Hygiene, Dora. Blimey you are a drip.

Dora Oh yes. Hygiene. I can kill all the nasty flies and bluebottles what come in through the window and spoil all your lovely food.

Macaroni Show me this miracle of science.

Dora Look out, Mr Macaroni there's a bluebockle now!

The audience all start to buzz

Wordsworth Blimey what a whopper!

Macaroni Do something—I can't stand bluebottles!

Dora Don't worry, Mr Macaroni, I'll get it.

Wordsworth Listen to that buzzing.

Nellie Get it, Dora. Use your——

All —diabolical dirty dishcloth!

Dora whips out her dishcloth. All the audience scream and die

Macaroni Magnifico! Completely dead! But you'll be glad to hear that I have a man from the Department of Health calling to see to all this problem. An expert, not a drippy twit! I shall not need you nor your silly cloth. You join Nellie at the end of the week.

Wordsworth Blimey that's a bit rough.

Macaroni Rough! Rough! I haven't started yet. (*Approaching Wordsworth*) Now what is your pathetic claim to fame eh? (*He is now nose to nose with Wordsworth*)

Wordsworth Well . . . er . . . er . . . Well I reckon I'm the very best waiter you've got. I can cope with any situation and any customer.

Macaroni Any situation and any customer eh? Well it happens that at this very moment I have some bigga important customers just arriving. They havea plenty money. They are very big and posherooji. You serve them OK you stay OK. OK?

Wordsworth OK.

Macaroni Ah I can hear them arriving now. You'd better be good.

Wordsworth I'm fantastic.

Macaroni We shall see.

Wordsworth tidies up his person and prepares for posh guests. Nellie and Dora take their hats and coats etc. as they enter. The following sequence must be done at high speed

Macaroni (*announcing*) The bigga film star. Miss Lolita Suspender.

Miss Lolita Suspender sweeps in, clad in fur coat

Wordsworth Cor. She's a cracker.

Lolita Hi there, you wonderful little kiddiewinkies.

Macaroni Brigadier Bumbracket.

Brigadier Bumbracket enters

Wordsworth (*snapping to attention and saluting*) Sir!

Bumbracket Stand at ease, my man. Right, sit up straight, all you spotty little herberts.

Macaroni Major Shareholder.

Major Shareholder enters

Wordsworth I bet he's rich.

Shareholder Here you are, my man. Two pence for a new teatowel.

Wordsworth Blimey, don't strain yourself, mate.

Macaroni Madame Dubonnet.

Madame Dubonnet enters

Wordsworth Oh cherie—you are so beautiful. (*He kisses her hand, wrist and arm*)

Dubonnet Ooo la la.

Dora and Nellie hand out food, plates and spoons to the customers

Macaroni Right, Wordsworth. They are all nicely settled. See that there are no problems.

Wordsworth Don't worry, my old spaghetti. I can deal with any kind of complaint.

The guests start slurping soup

Lolita Waiter, waiter. There's a horrible fly in my soup.
Wordsworth I'm terribly sorry, madam. The dog must have missed it.

Lolita screams and leaves

Bumbracket Why is this chop so terribly tough?
Wordsworth It's a karate chop, sir.
Bumbracket Good God!

Bumbracket exits

Shareholder Waiter, waiter. There's a bluebottle sitting on my potato.
Wordsworth I know, sir. It's the rotting meat that attracts them.
Shareholder Disgustin'.

Shareholder exits

Dubonnet Garçon, garçon. Zere is a spider swimming around in my soup.
Wordsworth Don't worry, madame. The goldfish will get it eventually.
Dubonnet Mon Dieu!

Dubonnet shrieks and exits

Macaroni WORDSWORTH!
Wordsworth Sir?
Macaroni You're FIRED!
Wordsworth Yes, sir. Thank you, sir.

Macaroni exits with a flourish

Nellie You've done it now, Wordsworth.
Dora I don't think he likes you, Wordsworth.
Wordsworth (*nearly in tears*) Never mind. We've found out one fing for certain.
Nellie 'Ave we?
Wordsworth Corst. (*Suddenly cheerful again*) He wants to expand. Get a bigga place.
Dora Get a bigga place.
Wordsworth So we've gotta help 'im.
Dora We've gotta 'elp 'im.
Nellie 'Ow d'you mean, Wordsworth?
Wordsworth Find someone wiv lots a money who likes 'im and who'll share their money wiv 'im.
Dora Share their money wiv 'im.
Nellie There's only one person who fancies Mr Macaroni.
Eileen (*off; in a stentorian voice*) Norman! It's time to open!
Norman (*off*) Yes, Auntie.
Dora You don't mean . . .?
Nellie That's exactly who I do mean.
Wordsworth Eileen "stuck-up" Nostril and her 'orrible little nephew Norman.
Dora (*dreamily*) I fink 'e's nice.
Nellie That's right. Eileen's crackers about old Macaroni.

Eileen (*off*) Norman! I am not in the habit of repeating myself.
Norman (*off*) Coming, Auntie.
Wordsworth Look out, 'ere she comes.
Nellie Let's try and devise a way of making her part with some of that money.
Wordsworth Get 'er to go into partnership with Macaroni. Whatja fink, Dora?
Dora I fink 'e's nice.
Wordsworth Who?
Dora Norman Nostril. 'E's got nice legs.
Wordsworth Wake up, Dora.
Nellie Get wiv it.
Eileen (*off; shrieking*) NORMAN!
Norman (*off; screaming*) I'm still putting me trousers on!
Wordsworth Quick, let's nip through to the kitchen and——

A Waiter pokes his head through the Pizza Pie Palace entrance

Waiter —put the kettle on.
All Put the kettle on——
Waiter —and have a nice cuppa tea.

The Waiter exits

All And have a nice cuppa tea.
Wordsworth Then down to the beach for a secret conflab.
Dora (*in a trance*) I dream about his trousers.
Nellie Oh come on, Dora!

Dora, Nellie and Wordsworth go into the Pizza Pie Palace and exit

Eileen and Norman Nostril enter from the Hairdressing Salon.

Eileen is loud, vulgar and flashily dressed in clothes that are far too young for her. She has an affected and assumed accent which she considers as "refeened" as her tasteless Hair Salon. Norman is a bit pathetic and wears a short-trousered suit and school cap. Eileen talks to him as if he were a dog and treats him as such. Normal pulls on a lady's hooded hair-drier on a stand. He also carries an appointments book. Eileen carries a tray on which we see razors, scissors and two saucers, one of foam and one of blacking. She puts the tray on the table. They then bring the two chairs forward

The Lights fade at the rear of the stage, creating a warm pink light DS *to capture the mood of the salon interior*

Eileen Norman.
Norman Yes, Auntie?
Eileen Sit! Now, Norman—listen very carefully. Are you listening?
Norman Yes, gorgeous Auntie.
Eileen (*flattered*) You know where the clean towels are?
Norman Yes, lovely Auntie.
Eileen Good—then fetch!

Norman scampers off to get them

Isn't he a good boy.

Norman scampers on with the towels

Norman (*giving them to her*) Here we are, Auntie. (*To the audience*) Sometimes Auntie gives me a lump of sugar if I'm good.
Eileen Good boy. (*She gives him a lump of sugar as if he were a horse and pats his head*) Now, Norman. Stay.

Norman freezes as she titivates the salon

Norman Auntie? (*He moves* R)
Eileen Yes, Normie?
Norman Auntie, can I have some long trousers soon?
Eileen (*freezing mid-work*) Don't be silly, Norman. You know very well that you are far too young to have long trousers.
Norman But I'm thirty-five, Auntie.
Eileen Exactly.
Norman But all my friends have got long trousers. (*He moves* L)
Eileen Norman! Heel!

He scuttles into a begging position

I don't want to hear any more of this silliness. Is that clear?
Norman Yes, Auntie. (*He pauses*) Albert Bogwort's got long trousers.
Eileen Norman. That is enough! We 'ave an 'igh-class salon to run.

Norman mimes the words with her

We 'ave queues of 'igh-class clientele waitin' to 'ave their wigs waved and their whiskers whipped orf. Do I make myself clear, Norman?
Norman Yes, fascinating creature.
Eileen Curb yourself, Norman and bring the appointment book.
Norman Yes Auntie, then we will know who our customers are today.

Norman brings the book. It contains the names and addresses of two children from the audience. These names were taken down by subterfuge as the children arrived in the auditorium. The boy and girl selected are oblivious of the fact that they are to be customers

(*Reading from the book*) Well Auntie, the next customers are (*girl's name and address*) and (*boy's name and address*).
Eileen Their names are most charmant. (*She sounds the "t"*) What cuts would they like?
Norman Well, (*girl*) would like the Eileen Nostril Funky Frizz and (*boy*) would like the Norman Nostril Short Sharp Shave and Shampoo.
Eileen Anything else, mon ami?
Norman Yes. I'd like a pair of long trousers.
Eileen Don't be stupid, Norman. (*She clouts him*) Now have you told them that they get a prize if they behave themselves?
Norman No.
Eileen Well?
Norman Well what?

Eileen Well, (*shouting*) tell them they get a nice prize if they behave themselves.

Norman Oh right. (*To the kids, shouting like Eileen*) You get a prize if you behave yourself. (*Now like himself*) Actually, you'll get one even if you muck about.

Norman starts laughing with the children. Eileen clouts him again

Eileen Norman. Sit! Stay! Now I want you to go and collect our clients and bring them into the salon. Ready . . . wait for it . . . fetch!

Norman goes into the audience, collects the kids and brings them on stage

Norman (*introducing them*) This is (*girl*). She wants to be a pop star or a long-distance lorry driver.

Eileen What a delightful young lady. Très chic.

Norman She's nice ain't she. (*He strokes her*)

Eileen All right. Don't be silly, Norman.

Norman Sorry, Auntie.

Eileen (*indicating the boy*) And who is this?

Norman This is (*boy*) and he wants to be a footballer or the Incredible Hulk's best friend.

Eileen Delighted to meet you (*boy*), mon petit.

Norman Seems like a nice boy.

Eileen Norman! Plug in the dryer.

Norman Sorry, Auntie. What shall I do now?

Eileen Sort out your scissors.

Norman Sort out your scissors.

Eileen Sharpen up your shaver.

Norman Sharpen up your shaver.

Eileen And start snipping the snippers.

Norman Start snipping the snippers.

SONG 2 (*Tune: Knees up Mother Brown*)

Eileen sprays the girl with perfume and drapes a towel over her clothes

Eileen   Head back if you please
                             Head back if you please
                             Under the drier you must go
                             Ee aye ee aye ee aye oh
                             If you start to fidget
                             We'll burn your hair right off
                             Then oh my gawdy
                             You'll be a baldy
                             Head back if you please.

Norman drapes a towel over the boy and starts to pretend to snip off bits of hair, clothing and anatomy

Norman   Chin up if you please
                             Chin up if you please

Under the scissors you must go
Ee aye ee aye ee aye oh
If you start to fidget
We'll clip your ears right off
So watch out, watch out
Pickin' all the fleas out
Chin up if you please.

Eileen ⎫   Oh my what a rotten song
Norman ⎭   What a rotten song, what a rotten song
                  Oh my what a rotten song

They pause as they sniff the smoke coming from the drier

And what a stinky pong as well.

They both scream as there is a flash and a Black-out as the drier explodes. During this Norman slaps shaving-foam or soot all over the boy's face, and Eileen over the girl's face

Eileen Emergency lights quickly.

The Lights come up to reveal the two kids covered in muck

Oh heavens, Norman, what on earth has happened?
Norman They've gone all funny.
Eileen Très catastroff. Quelle tragic! I shall never be able to hold my nose up in public again!
Norman Your nostrils are going all quivery, Auntie.
Eileen Oh no! A sign of impending disaster, Nephew Norman. What shall we do?
Norman We must make sure that our customers are fully compensated.
Eileen Talk properly, Norman. What do you mean?
Norman I mean we must see that (*girl*) and (*boy*) get a prize for being good. (*He turns to leave*)
Eileen Not so fast, Norman.
Norman (*speaking slowly*) I mean we must see that (*girl*) and (*boy*) get a prize for——
Eileen No, I mean don't act too rashly, Norm. First we must get 'em cleaned up before their 'orrible mums and dads see 'em in this state. Then we give them the prize——
Norman —to keep their mouths shut.
Eileen To keep their mouths shut.
Norman Good thinkin'.
Eileen And before they let everyone know that my salon is a load of old rubbish.
Norman But it *is* a load of old rubbish.
Eileen Of course it is, Normie, but we don't want everyone to know.
Norman (*bemused*) I don't understand that. I must be stupid.
Eileen Of course you are, Normie. The Nostril family have always been stupid.
Norman 'Ave they?

Eileen Since time immoral, Normie, and we'd like to keep it that way. Any more queries?

Norman Yes, Auntie . . . Can I 'ave a pair of long trousers?

Eileen (*haughtily ignoring his request*) Come, children—follow me.

Eileen escorts the children off stage where they are cleaned, given a prize and returned to their parents

Norman Blimey, poor old Auntie is ruined. All the machines are busted and all our money lost.

Dora begins to creep in

Which means that Auntie won't give me my pocket money and I was going to buy a packet of smokey bacon crisps to give to——

Dora 'Ello, Norman.

Norman Dora.

Dora I've just been down the beach wiv Wordsworth and Old Nellie.

Norman 'Ave you?

Dora Yeah—we've been conflabbin'.

Norman Is that good?

Dora Yeah—it's excitin'.

Norman I can think of something excitin', Dora.

Dora Can yer?

Norman Yeah.

Dora What?

Norman 'Oldin' your pandy.

Dora Your auntie wouldn't like it.

Norman My auntie ain't gonna do it.

Dora All right then.

They gingerly hold hands

Norman It's good, init?

Dora Yeah—smashin'. 'Ere Normie, 'ave you got 'oles in your trousers?

Norman No!

Dora 'Ow do you get your legs through like that then?

Norman Don't be drippy, Dora.

Dora I'm not. It's just that I dream about your legs.

Norman Do yer?

Dora Yeah—kneecaps mostly.

Norman Kneecaps?

Dora Mmmmmm.

Norman You can 'ave a feel if you like.

Dora What now?

Norman Yer. Corst.

Dora Cor ta! (*She is just about to have a feel*)

Wordsworth and Nellie enter

Nellie Dora!

Wordsworth What are you doin'?

Dora Nuffin'.
Norman She was checkin' my legs.
Wordsworth Well, he's got two, Dora—OK?
Nellie Cor. There ain't 'alf a pong in here.
Wordsworth Like something's been burning, Nellie.
Norman Yeah. Auntie has blown up all the machines. We're broke.
Wordsworth Skint?
Nellie Penniless?
Dora Soft down?
Wordsworth Hard up, Dora!
Dora Oh yeah.
Nellie 'Ere 'old on.
All 'Old on.
Nellie I think our employment problems 've been answered, Wordsworth.
Wordsworth Wonder-Granny brain-power?
Nellie Right. Norman's auntie has lost all her money. She's gonna need a partner.
Wordsworth Mr Macaroni!
Nellie He'll buy up her premises so he can expand the Pizza Palace and——
Wordsworth —he'll need extra staff so——
Dora —we keep our jobs.
Wordsworth Exactly, Dora. We keep our jobs.
Nellie Not bad eh? Hee hee hee.
Wordsworth Not bad! It's scintillific! I must start eating up all my greens.
Norman But I don't think my auntie will want to give up her hairdressing.
Nellie She will if we can convince her that there's more money in pizza pies——
Wordsworth (*going dreamy*) —and fish 'n' chips——
Dora —and mushrooms——
Norman —and long trousers.

They all clout him

Nellie Knock it off, Norman. She's got to see that there's a rosy future in the restaurant business.
Wordsworth What we need is someone who could make her believe that she'd make a fortune in pizzas.
Norman Who could do that?
Dora A fortune teller.
Wordsworth But where are we going to get one of those?
Nellie (*indicating the audience*) Maybe they'll 'elp.

The kids in the audience draw their attention to the posters on stage and in the auditorium advertising "FATIMA PHILPOT—FAMOUS FORTUNE TELLER"

(*Reading it*) "Fatima Philpot—Famous Fortune Teller."
Wordsworth Of course. Fatty Philpot! Quick, nip down to the pier and fetch her, Dora.

Nellie It's no good going.
Dora No good?
Nellie No. She's gone to visit Big Beryl in Bournemouth.
Wordsworth 'Ere. Not to worry.
All Not to worry!
Wordsworth Does your auntie know Fatty Philpot, Norman?
Nellie No. She's frightened of foreigners.
Wordsworth Good. Then I could disguise myself as Fatty Philpot.
Nellie And I could pretend to be 'er mystical snake, Albert.
Norman And I could fetch Auntie Eileen here.
Dora And I could lend you my pencil.
Wordsworth What *would* we do without you, Dora?
Nellie OK. Action stations.

They start to get ready for the fortune-telling sequence. Nellie brings on a huge jar and sets it DR. *She gets inside the jar and puts a snake sock over her arm. Wordsworth brings on a tablecloth and a crystal ball and puts them on the table after pulling it forward. Dora brings on pinafores and teatowels with which they disguise themselves as Arabian mystics. Norman goes off to look for Eileen*

Norman (*as he goes*) Auntie. Auntie. Where are you? There's a fortune-teller lady wants to see you . . . about the future.

Norman exits

Dora (*to the kids*) Oh I nearly forgot. Will you make a hissing noise when Albert the snake appears? Wordsworth asked especially. Ta. Good this, init? Ready Wordsworth?
Wordsworth (*now dressed as a woman*) Right. Let's get in the mood.

We hear Eastern music and the Lights take on a darker Arabian hue. Wordsworth and Dora do a silly Eastern dance until we hear Norman talking to Eileen

Norman (*off*) This way, Auntie.

Norman and Eileen enter

Eileen But who is this lady, Norman?
Norman She's a fortune teller, Auntie.
Eileen I hope she's not foreign.
Norman Only a little bit, Auntie.
Wordsworth (*in a woman's high-pitched voice*) Welcome, mystic creature.
Dora Mystic creature.
Eileen Ooo I say—that's rather nice isn't it, Normie?
Norman Very nice, Auntie.
Wordsworth What secret knowledge do you seek, O siren of the shampoo?
Dora Shampoo.
Eileen (*trying to get the feel of the atmosphere*) I wouldst knowest my future. I didn't catch the name?
Wordsworth I didn't throw it. I mean . . . Fatima.

Eileen Oh, very nice. (*She sniffs—it's foreign*) Wellst Fatima, I wouldst knowest what may becometh of me-est.

Wordsworth You wouldst look into the womb of time?

Dora The tomb of wine?

Eileen Yes please-est.

Wordsworth Then cross my palm with fifty p.

Norman You have to give her some silver, Auntie.

Eileen Oh really? Well all I've got left is five p.

Wordsworth (*snatching it*) That will do, stingy.

Eileen (*taken aback*) What!?

Wordsworth I feel the present drifting away.

Dora Away.

Wordsworth I can see the days and years to come, swimming before my orbs.

Dora Orbs.

Eileen Good heavens, how dreadful.

Wordsworth (*suddenly and loudly*) The mist is clearing.

Dora It's gonna be a nice day.

Wordsworth It's gonna be a nice—it's much clearer than it was before. What's this I see?

Eileen What is it?

Wordsworth (*screaming*) Aaaaaaah!

All (*screaming*) Aaaaaaah!

Norman What is it? What is it?

Wordsworth It's . . . Albert.

Eileen Albert?

Wordsworth It's Albert.

Dora The mystic snake.

Wordsworth Spirit of the East.

Eileen What does it want?

Wordsworth It has a message.

Eileen Oh my gawd.

Norman It's got a message for you, Auntie.

Eileen I can't see a snake.

Wordsworth Watch and you will see.

Dora You will see.

A snake appears out of the basket. It is Nellie's arm inside a snake sleeve—it has crossed eyes and looks at the audience

Eileen Oh, my heavens, it's . . . it's——

Norman —'orrible, Auntie.

Eileen It's . . . it's——

Wordsworth —Albert. Ask and Albert will answer.

Norman Ask him who you're going to marry, Auntie.

Eileen I feel soppy asking a snake something like that.

Wordsworth Have no fears. Look deep into Albert's eyes and you will hear the answers to all your questions.

Dora Albert will hypno-surprise you.

Eileen This is silly. I don't believe in hypno—— (*She suddenly goes rigid*)

The others all hum

(*Trance-like*) Whom will I marry?

Nellie (*like a snake*) Mr Macaroni.

Eileen That ist good. Will I be rich?

Nellie Beyond your wildest dreamssssss.

Eileen That ist even gooderest.

Wordsworth Albert. (*In one breath*) Should Auntie Eileen sell her hair-dressing salon to Mr Macaroni so he can go into partnership with her and extend his Pizza Pie Palace, thus enabling any unfortunates that have been deprived of their jobs to be re-employed in the restaurant and live happily ever after?

Nellie Yesssssss.

Wordsworth Good.

Eileen Canst I have a fur coat?

Wordsworth Albert grows tired.

Dora It's time for his cocoa.

Wordsworth It's time for his—it's time that he left. When I clap my hands you will awake, and will remember everything except the silly bits.

Dora Except the silly bits.

They quickly whip off their disguises and Nellie comes out of the snake jar

Eileen Oh what a shame. There were so many questions I wanted to——

Wordsworth claps. The Lights come up again

—ask him. (*She comes out of her hypnotic trance*)

Wordsworth Hello, Miss Nostril.

Eileen Ooo! Ooo my goodness me. I feel all funny peculiar. I must have been dreaming.

Dora You were hypno-surprised.

Nellie Don't you remember?

Eileen I do, I do.

Norman She does, she does.

Nellie I'm glad, 'cos 'ere comes Mr Macaroni.

Eileen Heavens, I must look a fright. Kneecap, Normie.

Norman lifts his kneecap which Eileen uses as a mirror to fix her face

Mr Macaroni enters

Macaroni (*as he sweeps in*) Miss Nostrila—I've been looking for you everywhere.

Eileen Oh, Mr Macaroni. You've no idea what I've been through.

Dora She's been hypno-surprised.

Eileen I've been hypno-thingy and I have lost all my money.

Macaroni Don't worry . . . Eileeno.

Eileen Cooo!

Nellie Saucy monkey!

Macaroni I shall help you.

Norman He's gonna help you, Auntie.

Macaroni I will buy your establishment and then extend my ristorante . . . then . . . it would give me great pleasure if you would become my partner . . . permanento. What is your answer?

Eileen Oh . . . Marcello . . . I don't know what to say. Yes!

All Hurrah.

Macaroni Soon I will be able to buy the whole street. (*He is very pleased with himself*)

Wordsworth The whole street?

Nellie What you been up to Mr Macaroni?

Dora He's done a deal.

Macaroni Exactimunto. I've donna the big deal.

Norman Oooh. Sounds exciting.

Eileen Let us all into the secret, Marcello.

Macaroni I've just been very lucky.

Wordsworth Lucky?

Macaroni Si. I bought this priceless treasure map for only five thousand smackeroojis. (*He produces a map*)

Nellie Let's 'ave a look.

Dora Cor, treasure.

Wordsworth Oh no!!!

Macaroni There's something wrong?

Wordsworth I'll say there's something wrong.

Eileen What's the matter?

Wordsworth I'm afraid you've been done, my old marshmallow.

Macaroni Done?

Wordsworth Yes. Who did you buy this map from?

Macaroni There is something wrong with the map?

Wordsworth I should say there's something wrong. It's a map of the London Underground.

All Oh no!

Macaroni But I bought it from a very nice old oriental gentleman down by the harbour.

Dora Nice?

Nellie Old?

Wordsworth Oriental?

Norman Gentleman?

Macaroni Down by the harbour?

Eileen (*nearly passing out*) Oh my gawd. It can't be?

Wordsworth It can be.

Nellie It is.

Wordsworth Captain Kung Fu and the Wing Wangs!

Macaroni You donta mean the dreaded pirate, Captain Kung Fu.

Wordsworth That's exactly who I do mean.

Nellie He must've been using one of his disguises.

Dora (*bravely*) Don't worry, Mr Macaroni, we'll get it back.

Norman (*to the audience*) She's nice, ain't she.

Macaroni All my money lost!

Eileen We're ruined—ruined!

Nellie We'll get after 'em straight away.

Wordsworth Norman!·

Nellie Yes, Wordsworth.

Wordsworth You take care of Auntie Eileen.

Nellie Right. Come on, Auntie, and I'll get you a nice gin and tonic.

Wordsworth Macaroni—you see to all these customers. See that they get a free pizza.

Macaroni Okey dokey.

Wordsworth While——

Nellie —Old Nellie——

Dora —Drippy Dora——

Wordsworth —and I Wordsworthy One, hunt down——

All —Captain Kung Fu and the Wing Wangs.

Nellie, Norman, Eileen, Dora and Wordsworth tear off stage

Macaroni OK. The pizzas are on me!!!

CURTAIN

ACT II

The House Lights go down quite quickly and the stage floods with blue. Piratical Chinese junk blocks are set on stage. There is danger about. Suddenly Chinese cymbals and crashes are heard, accompanied by vocalized "chinky" hullabaloo

Captain Kung Fu enters, flourishing a cutlass. He has a crutch, a horribly spotty face, a dead parrot on his shoulder (or possibly two or three, one of which is skeletal) and a Kung Fu scarf round his forehead

The dreaded Wing Wangs accompany him. They plough in amongst the audience, generally cursing and blaspheming in Wing-Wang talk. To "wing-wang" someone means to flick a Chinese sword-stick at them (see diagram on page 39)

Kung Fu (*blowing a whistle*) All Wing-Wang crew on deck vellee quickee.
Wangs Ah, ay, slipper!
Kung Fu All abloard the *Jolly Lodger.*
Wangs Kung Fu calls.

The Lights change to a warm pink, as the Wing Wangs rush up on to the stage making chinky sounds. During the next sequence they build the "Jolly Lodger" from the blocks

Kung Fu Splice the flied lice!
Wangs Splice the flied lice!
Kung Fu Swab the chop-suey!
Wangs Swab the chop-suey!
Kung Fu Sing sillee songee!!
Wangs Sing sillee songee!!

SONG 3 (*Tune: What Shall We Do With The Drunken Sailor?*)

Oh what shall we do with naughty children?
Oh what shall we do with naughty children?
Oh what shall we do with naughty children?
Earlie in the morning?

Make 'em walk the plank and give 'em a wing-wang

They flick out their Chinese sword-sticks

Make 'em walk the plank and give 'em a wing-wang
Make 'em walk the plank and give 'em a wing-wang
Earlie in the morning.

Kung Fu Shiver me chopsticks! Cap'n Kung Fu is vellee pleased with day's work.
Wangs Goodee. Goodee.
Kung Fu We foolee Macaroni.
Wong Eye Grabbee.
Wong Arm Lotsee.
Wong Leg Lovelee.
Numb Bum Monee.
Kung Fu Now to workee. Wun Wong Eye.
Wong Eye Captain.
Kung Fu Check the shippee.
Wong Eye Ay, ay, Cap'n.

Wun Wong Eye exits

Kung Fu Wun Numb Bum.
Numb Bum Captain.
Kung Fu Prepare chicken for dinner.
Numb Bum Slate away, Captain.

Wun Numb Bum exits

Kung Fu Wun Wong Arm, Wun Wong Leg. Guard all these nastee little piggies—*(referring to the audience)*—and if they give any trouble . . .
Wangs Wing Wang!

Wun Wong Eye enters carrying a pathetic piece of shredded rubber

Wong Eye Captain, trouble on board.
Kung Fu What trouble?
Wong Eye Inflatable rubber dinghy collapsed and died, Captain.
Kung Fu Patch it!
Wong Eye *(removing his eye-patch)* Right away, Captain.

Wung Wong Eye exits

Wun Numb Bum enters

Numb Bum Captain, chicken plucked and stuffed ready for dinner.
Kung Fu Excellent. Now kill it and cook it.
Numb Bum I go vellee quick.

Wun Numb Bum exits

Wong Arm What we do today, Captain?
Wong Leg Catch fishee?
Wong Arm Sun bathee?
Wong Leg Muck aboutee?
Kung Fu No! Somethin' more excitee.

Wun Numb Bum and Wun Wong Eye hear this and enter

Wangs More excitee?
Kung Fu Yes. I have brilliant plan!
Wangs Oooooo.
Wong Arm Captain Kung Fu vellee glate man.
Wong Leg When he born——

Wong Eye —they fire twenty-one guns.
Numb Bum Unfortunately all missee!

They all cackle and wing-wang the audience

Kung Fu (*angrily*) No jokee!
Wangs No jokee!
Kung Fu My plan is to escape with monee that Mr Macaroni give us for soppee map——
Wangs Vellee good. Vellee good.
Kung Fu —to sail the seven soya sauces and search for safe hiding place——
Wangs Vellee good. Vellee good.
Kung Fu —where we can have vellee good time spending money on ice creams and space-invader machines.
Wangs Yippee! *etc.* (*They go berserk, tee-heeing and wing-wanging ad lib*)
Kung Fu But!
Wangs But?
Kung Fu The question is where we sail to?
Wong Eye I go to China once.
Wong Foot Vellee interlesting?
Wong Eye Vellee disapplointing.
Wong Foot Reason?
Wong Eye Early closing day.
Wangs Aaaaah.
Numb Bum Captain I know of vellee safe place, where no-one find us.
Kung Fu This sound good.
Numb Bum Yes—it where my sister, Beryl live.
Kung Fu Beryl?
Numb Bum Yes, she own big bloarding house.
Kung Fu What this paradise called?
Numb Bum It call—Blournemouth.
Wangs Blournemouth.
Kung Fu Crispy Cutlass—this sound excellent spot. Your sister vellee rich?
Numb Bum No she vellee poor—made in Hong Kong—but she make vellee good chop-suey.
Kung Fu Then we shall sail for Blournemouth.
Wangs Wing Wang!
Kung Fu But first we must get Macaroni's money on board.
Wong Arm And plenty of gunpowdee in case we are attacked.
Wong Foot And plenty of foodee for the journey.
Kung Fu Wun Wong Eye you will stay here on guard. Keep an eye on things.
Wong Eye Yes, Captain.
Kung Fu And remember no boozing or snoozing.
Wong Eye Certainly not, Captain.
Kung Fu Vellee wellee, the rest of you follow Kung Fu. Get money, food and gunpowder!!

Wangs Wing Wang!

All except Wun Wong Eye exit, jabbering about gunpowder, food and money

Wong Eye Ah. Now Captain out of slight I can have little drinkee. Wun Wong Eye's favourite boozee. Lucozadee! (*He produces a large bottle from behind one of the blocks and drinks, making scrummy noises*) Vellee delicious. Now you lot all stay still. No try and escape. No try funny business while I have short sharp snoozee. (*He settles down and begins to snore*)

Wordsworth, Nellie and Dora enter the auditorium. They are wearing oilskins and big sou'wester hats. Dora is carrying a big parcel marked "PIZZA"

Wordsworth Come on, Nellie. This is where Cap'n Kung Fu usually leaves his boat.
Nellie Don' go so fast, Wordsworth.
Dora (*jumping*) My legs are gettin' all mixed up.
Wordsworth Just try and use one at a time, Dora.

Dora stops jumping and puts one foot in front of the other

Dora Oh yeah, it's easier this way, init.
Wordsworth Wotcher bring that for? (*He points to the parcel*)
Dora In case we get hungry.
Nellie (*stopping as she spots the guard*) 'Ere 'old on.
Wordsworth ⎫
Dora ⎭ (*together*) 'Ere 'old on.
Nellie That looks like one of Kung Fu's Wing Wangs.
Dora I wonder what he's doin' there.
Wordsworth We'll ask the children. See if they know anything about him.
Nellie Oh yes. 'Ere what's 'is name?

They extract from the audience the name Wun Wong Eye

Dora Wun Wonky Eye. Yeah, but what's he doin' sleepin' there?

They extract from the audience that he is on guard

Wordsworth On guard, eh. But where 'ave Captain Kung Fu and the others disappeared to?
Nellie 'Ave they gone to get anything?

They extract from the audience that the Wing Wangs have gone to collect the food, money and gunpowder

Wordsworth Collecting the money. We must get that back for Mr Macaroni.
Nellie And gunpowder. Nasty stuff that.
Dora And food. Nice stuff that.
Wordsworth Nellie my old jelly baby. I think this situation calls for——
Nellie —action stations.

Wordsworth 'Ere, children, what do you think we ought to do about Wun Wong Eye?
Nellie Yeah. How can we get rid of him?
Dora Bump 'im off?

The kids will suggest all sorts of things. Use their ideas and carry them out. They might say use Dora's diabolical dishcloth, or pinch his Lucozade or stab him with a dagger or bash 'im over the head with a big sausage. Improvize the slaughter

Right. That's done 'im under.
Nellie One down.
Wordsworth Five to go, Nellie.
Nellie 'Ow do you know there's only five left, Wordsworth?
Wordsworth I'll tell you 'ow I know, Nellie. I can see 'em comin' this way, right now!
Dora Oh no, King Kong's comin' back.
Wordsworth We'd better hide.
Nellie Quick—the kids'll help us. Under the tables.
Wordsworth Below decks.

They hide among the audience

Dora (*bobbing up*) It's good this, init.
Wordsworth
Nellie } (*together; insistently*) GET DOWN DORA!!

The Wing Wangs enter singing "What shall we do with all the money" etc. They are carrying boxes and a barrel of gunpowder. The boxes are labelled with their contents and each is clearly marked "By Appointment to Her Majesty's Pirates". Kung Fu carries a big box of money

Kung Fu Vellee good. Now load gunpowder on board. Stolen food over there.
Wong Arm (*lifting a box*) Cream doughnuts!
Wangs Gobsloppers!
Wong Foot Ice lollies!
Numb Bum Frozen chop-suey!
Kung Fu (*looking inside the boxes*) Oh no, you stupid noodles! These only sample boxes. Food inside no good at all.
Wangs No good at all.
Kung Fu Of course no good. Not real food. Only made of cardboard for shop windees.
Wong Foot Oh dearie. Now we be vellee hungry on voyage.
Kung Fu Serve you jollee well rightee, Chinese Crackerjack.

Wordsworth, Dora and Nellie leap out of hiding

Wangs
Wordsworth
Dora } (*together*) CRACKERJACK!
Nellie

Wordsworth, Dora and Nellie go straight back into hiding

Kung Fu Where is Wun Wong Eye?
Wong Arm Almost certainly gone for quick boozie.
Wong Leg At *Pig and Crispy Pancake*.
Kung Fu Stupid ninny. But we not care. We have bigger share of money. We sail without him.
Dora What a rotten bloke.
Kung Fu What a rotten bloke. Who say that?
Wangs (*suspicious*) Who say that?
Dora (*standing up*) I did.
Wangs (*pointing at her and relaxing*) She did. (*Double-take*) She did!
Kung Fu Get her quickee.

A chase ensues. Wordsworth, Dora and Nellie are eventually captured and led up on to the stage

Kung Fu Wing Wangs, cover all exits.
Wangs Wing Wang! (*They cover all exits*)
Kung Fu You three line up over there.

Wordsworth, Dora and Nellie go through the earlier Macaroni sequence

     You speakee the truth and——
All —and——
Kung Fu —I might let you go free.
Dora He's quite nice, in'e?
Kung Fu You, what is your namee?
Dora (*stepping forward*) Dora, Mr Kung Poo, sir. Drippy Dora.
Kung Fu What?
Wordsworth She's a loony sir.
Kung Fu And what is your name?
Wordsworth Wordsworth, sir.
Kung Fu What kind of a name is this?
Wordsworth My dad liked chop-suey, sir.
Nellie And I'm Nellie, Nellie——
Wordsworth —with the big fat——
Kung Fu What?
Wordsworth —kneecaps, sir. She's got very big kneecaps.
Kung Fu OK. You think yourself pretty smart bamboo shoots—but soon you will be walking the gangplankee.
All Walk the plank? Oh no.

The Wing Wangs prepare the gangplank which extends off the edge of the stage into the audience

Nellie Seaweed.
Wordsworth Sharks.
Dora Davy Jones' knickers.
Wordsworth (*bravely*) Don't worry, Nellie. Don't worry, Dora. You can depend on me.
Kung Fu (*to Wordsworth*) You first.

Wordsworth Go on, Nellie. I'm right behind you.

Kung Fu No you.

Wordsworth Oh Dora, of course. Show us how it's done, Dora.

Kung Fu No YOU!

Wordsworth Me? Those sharks won't like me.

Dora 'E tastes 'orrible.

Wordsworth I taste 'orrible—do you mind, Dora.

Kung Fu Come along now—please walkee this way.

Nellie Goodbye, Wordsworth. Be brave—you'll never live to regret it.

Wordsworth (*nearly in tears*) Thank you, Nellie.

Dora Goodbye, Wordsworth—would you like to take my pencil wiv you?

Wordsworth No, Dora—I think I'll be able to manage on my own.

Kung Fu Hully up please. Sharkees velly hunglee.

Numb Bum Time for tea.

Kung Fu Any last requests?

Wordsworth Yes. I'd like to sing "Six million green bottles hanging on the wall". (*He starts to do so*)

Kung Fu Enough sillee talkee! Start walkee!

Wordsworth Enough sillee talkee, start walkee. I don' wanna die.

Nellie Be brave, Wordsworth.

Wordsworth (*walking the gangplank*) I'm trying but it's difficult when you're a coward. Aagh. Look at their teeth.

Kung Fu Five steps please.

Dora He was the best waiter Mr Macaroni ever had.

Wangs Floor, flea, two, one.

Kung Fu Stop!

Wordsworth Aaaagh!

Kung Fu Did you say waitee?

Dora Yes, Wordsworth's fantastic.

Nellie And he can cook!

Kung Fu Good cookee eh? Just what we wantee.

Wordsworth Do yer?

Kung Fu Yes. Only cardboard food for long voyage to Blournemouth. You make us something to eat—we not feed you to sharkee.

Nellie I'm good at sums, Mr Kung Fu. I could work out how to divide up your treasure into fair shares like.

Dora And I could kill all the rats on board with my diabolical dirty dish-cloth.

Kung Fu Mmmm. Vellee good. I give you trial, while we go below deck and have small snoozee. Here is gold, there is cooking pot and rats are everywhere.

Dora Nasty.

Kung Fu Start workee.

Kung Fu exits

All Ay, ay, Cap'n.

Wong Arm Haul up anchor.

Wong Leg Let go ropee.

Wong Foot You start cookee.
Numb Bum We go snoozee.

The Wing Wangs exit, cackling

Wordsworth Blimey, that was a narrow squeak.
Nellie I didn't fancy being a sharkburger.
Dora Nor me.
Nellie We're in a fix now, Wordsworth.
Wordsworth I don't know what I can find to cook for that rotten lot.
Dora I wish Normie was here to protect me.
Wordsworth Normie! He couldn't protect a chip from a frying-pan.
Dora 'E could. He can crack walnuts wiv his kneecaps.
Nellie All very interesting Dora, but I think we'd better 'ave a serious——
Wordsworth —conflab.
All Right. (*They move into a huddle*)
Nellie Point one, they're hungry.
Wordsworth Point two, we ain't got nuffin' to feed 'em with.
Dora Point three, I've brought a giant pizza wiv me.
Wordsworth
Nellie }(*together*) Point three, she's brought a giant pizza wiv 'er.
Nellie Brilliant, Dora!
Wordsworth Magnificent, Dora! Didn't you ever realize that you've got a brain?
Dora Never entered me 'ead.
Nellie Using my Wonder-Granny brain-power, I've just come up with a treble greens-graded idea.
Wordsworth What, Nellie?
Nellie Well, we've got to escape—supposing we put something in the pizza that would knock out all those Wing Wangs.
Dora My dishcloth!
Wordsworth No, that pongs too much. They'd be suspicious.
Dora Oh yeah.
Nellie I wonder if the young 'uns have any ideas as to what we could bung in the pizza?

They get the audience round to suggesting the gunpowder

Wordsworth Of course. The gunpowder. Very nasty, explosive pizza pie.
Nellie That'll give 'em indigestion.
Wordsworth Wait a minute.
All Wait a minute.
Wordsworth That'll never work. The gunpowder wouldn't explode.
Dora (*producing a box of matches*) It would if you put matches inside.
Wordsworth It would if we put matches inside. Dora, you get more brilliant hour by hour.
Nellie Right, action stations. Unwrap the pizza, Dora.

Dora opens the box, and they prepare the pizza

Wordsworth I'll get the gunpowder.

Nellie I'll put the matches inside.
Wordsworth I'll sprinkle the gunpowder on.
Dora And I'll cut it into five slices.
Wordsworth That's one more than four, Dora.
Dora Right.
Nellie Look at that. Really appetizing, init.

Dora goes to nibble it

Wordsworth Don't be a 'nana, Dora. You'll blow yourself sky-high.
Nellie I'll go and give them a shout.
Wordsworth Right, Nellie.
Nellie (*shouting off*) Grub up!
Wordsworth Now Nellie, I reckon it'll take about twenty-five seconds
  before the slices explode.
Nellie Blimey, it won't arf muck up their insides.
Wordsworth Liquidate their livers.
Dora Transmogrify their tripes.
Nellie Don't be filthy, Dora.
Dora Sorry.

Kung Fu and the Wing Wangs enter, carrying bibs

Kung Fu (*as he enters*) Ah so you make foodee, vellee quickee.
Wangs Vellee good, vellee good.
Wordsworth Yes Captain Kung Fu, we think you'll like this.
Dora It's got explosives in.
Wordsworth It's got ex—tra special things inside.
Nellie Take your places please.
Kung Fu (*to Wing Wangs*) Bibbees on please.
Wangs Bibbees on. (*They put on their bibs*)
Dora Din din is served.

They each take a slice of the explosive pizza pie

Wordsworth OK.
Nellie Start to——
Dora —munchee.
Wordsworth Five.
Nellie Four.
Dora Two.
Wordsworth One.
All Bingo!

*There is a gigantic explosion, a Black-out and smoke accompanied by
horrible screams. During this the Pirates strike the ship and re-set as in
ACT I and in the darkness we hear . . .*

Nellie I've got Mr Macaroni's money, Wordsworth.
Wordsworth Well done, Nellie. 'Ere where's Dora?
Nellie
Wordsworth }(*together*) Dora!

Dora 'Old on I gotta get sunnink important.
Nellie 'Urry up, Dora.
Wordsworth Right. Overboard and swim for your life.
All Swim for your life!

As the smoke clears, the Lights come up and we are back on shore outside Macaroni's ristorante. Wordsworth, Nellie and Dora are swimming on the floor

Wordsworth Keep going.

Dora is swimming like a loony, doing a back crawl

Nellie It's getting shallower.
Wordsworth It's getting drier.

Wordsworth and Nellie slow down as they realize they are back safely

Nellie 'Ere, we've made it, Wordsy.
Wordsworth So we have.

He spots Dora still swimming

  OK, Dora, we've made it.
Nellie   ⎫
Wordsworth ⎬ *(together)* Dora!
Dora *(continuing to swim)* What?
Nellie   ⎫
Wordsworth ⎬ *(together)* We're back!
Dora *(stopping)* Oh yeah.
Nellie Nice to be home, init.
Wordsworth Nice to be safe.
Dora Nice to have Norman near.
Norman *(off)* Dora, Dora.
Wordsworth How did you know he was comin', Dora?
Dora Extra sensory conception.
Wordsworth ⎫
Nellie   ⎬ *(together; bemused)* Oh.

  Norman enters

Norman 'Ello, Dora. You got back all right then?
Dora Yeah, we blew up Captain Kung Fu's tummy. It weren't 'arf good.
Wordsworth And I had to walk the plank.
Norman Crikey.
Nellie And I got all Mr Macaroni's money back.
Norman Cor that really is smashin'.
Wordsworth Where is Mr Macaroni?
Norman He's gettin' the wedding ring.
Nellie Wedding ring?
Norman Yeah, he's gonna marry my Auntie Eileen.
Dora Where's she, Normie?
Norman She's upstairs gettin' her torso ready.

Wordsworth Trousseau, Norman.
Norman Yeah, that as well.

Mr Macaroni enters, wearing a morning-suit

Macaroni Ah my friends, so you havea returned.
Nellie Returned and retrieved all your money, Mr Macaroni. (*She gives it to him*)
Macaroni Excellent! Now I can really expand. I shall open a completely new restaurant.
Wordsworth And . . . er . . . what about us, Mr Macaroni?
Macaroni (*mock stern*) What about you! You will be . . . my three new head waiters.
All Great!
Nellie Does that mean I get a new cardy?
Macaroni A new cardy, Nellie and bigger wages.
Dora Cor thanks very much, Mr Zavaroni.
Macaroni No no! I should thanka you for all your help.
Wordsworth And all the boys and girls as well.
Macaroni Oh yes—(*to the audience*)—thank you all very much indeed.
Nellie I hear there's going to be a wedding, Mr Macaroni.
Macaroni (*shy*) Exactimunto . . . and today is the day.
Eileen (*off; singing*) I'm getting married to Marcello
                              Ding dong the bells are gonna ring
                              So pull out the stoppa
                              And let's have a whoppa . . .

Eileen enters from the auditorium in a wedding dress

There is "musica romantica" played

Macaroni Eileeno.
Eileen Marcello.
Macaroni You looka so breathtaking.
Eileen Really?
Macaroni Si. You remind me of that beautiful Italian dish.
Eileen Sophia Loren.
Macaroni No—spaghetti.

Everyone laughs

Eileen (*coming on stage*) Oh really Marcello. You little Mediterranean tinker.
Macaroni Eileeno. You I adore.
All Aaaah.
Dora Why don't you say those three little words to me, Normie?
Norman What? Blow your nose?
Dora No. I mean can't I feel your heart beating?
Norman Why, ain'tcher got one of yer own?
Wordsworth I fink Dora wants you to propose, Normie.
Nellie 'E ain't old enough.
Wordsworth What's it say on the label of your underpants, Normie?

Norman (*looking*) Seven to eight years old.

Wordsworth That's old enough.

Norman Is it?

Nellie ⎫
Wordsworth ⎬ (*together*) Course it is.

Norman All right then, Dora.

Dora (*side by side with Norman*) Cor. I'll be able to 'old your pandy all the time now, won' I?

Norman Yeah.

Macaroni (*side by side with Eileen*) And I shall havea your love, Eileeno, for all eternity.

Eileen Oh Marcello.

Nellie (*suddenly snuggling up to Wordsworth*) Turning out quite nice, init, Wordsy?

Wordsworth Oh my gawdfathers! (*He hastily runs across the stage to conduct a quick ceremony*) Dearly beloved, we are gathered here safely away from Captain Kung Fu and the Wing Wangs——

There is a wing-wang cry off, and the Wing Wangs whistle in from the wings

——to join this man, this woman, this loony and this thingy. Do you promise to do all the things that people do when they get married?

All We do.

Wordsworth Good. I now pronounce you man, wife, loony and (*looking at Norman*) thingy. Bring on the cakes and the wedding presents! (*He throws confetti over them*)

The Waiters bring on presents and the wedding cake

Eileen Presents? Oo, lovely.

Macaroni Yes, my petal, here, I buy you a new food mixer. (*He gives her a wooden spoon*)

Eileen (*disappointed*) Oh, very nice.

Wordsworth It's the thought that counts.

Dora I got sunnink for you, Normie.

Norman Not a——

Dora Yes, a pair of long trousers. (*She hands him a pair*)

Norman For me?

Dora Your very own—they got 'oles in too.

Eileen Lovely, Dora. You must have been saving up a long time to be able to buy those.

Dora No, I nicked 'em off the pirates.

Nellie Little rascal.

Norman Cor thanks, Dora.

Norman and Dora kiss

Macaroni And now everyone is invited to the wedding breakfast.

Wordsworth What's it gonna be, Mr Macaroni?

Nellie (*miserably*) Pizza pie, I expect.

Macaroni No today we have fish and chipperies.

All HURRAH!

They sing a reprise of the pizza pie song (Song 1). During this, the cake candles are lit, more presents are opened, balloons descend from above and streamers are thrown. The Company dance and sing, as——

the CURTAIN *falls*

FURNITURE AND PROPERTY LIST

ACT I

On stage: White patio table with umbrella shade. *On it:* four plates and spoons, "food"
   2 white chairs
   Menu slate and chalk
   2 "FATIMA PHILPOT" posters
   Gangplank projecting into audience

In auditorium: "FATIMA PHILPOT" posters

Off stage: Hair-drier (with pre-set flash-pot) on wheeled stand **(Norman)**
   Appointments book **(Norman)**
   Tray with 2 razors, 2 pairs of scissors, perfume spray, 1 saucer of blacking, 1 saucer of foam **(Eileen)**
   2 towels **(Norman)**
   Snake jar, snake sleeve **(Nellie)**
   Tablecloth, crystal ball **(Wordsworth)**
   Pinafores, teatowels **(Dora)**

Personal: **Waiters:** teatowels, notepads, pencils
   Macaroni: whistle, carnation in buttonhole
   Dora: notepad, clip-on pencils, school report, filthy rag
   Nellie: hair-net, question paper
   Lolita: dark glasses
   Bumbracket: monocle
   Shareholder: cane, 2p coin
   Dubonnet: cigarette holder
   Eileen: lump of sugar, 5p coin
   Macaroni: map

ACT II

On stage: Chinese junk blocks
   Large bottle labelled "LUCOZADEE" (concealed) (for **Wun Wong Eye**)
   Gangplank projecting into audience

During the Black-out on page 29, the Chinese junk is struck and the stage re-set as in Act I

Off stage: Piece of shredded rubber **(Wun Wong Eye)**
   Large parcel labelled "PIZZA". *In it:* 5 pizza slices **(Dora)**
   4 coloured boxes labelled "CREAM DOUGHNUTS", "GOB-

SLOPPERS", "ICE LOLLIES", "FROZEN CHOP-SUEY"; each is also labelled "By Appointment to Her Majesty's Pirates" **(Wing Wangs)**

Barrel of gunpowder **(Wing Wangs)**

Big box of money **(Kung Fu)**

Bibs **(Wing Wangs)**

Wedding cake with candles, assorted wedding presents, streamers, wooden spoon for **Macaroni**, pair of long trousers for **Dora (Waiters)**

Balloons **(Stage Management)**

Personal: **Kung Fu:** cutlass, dead parrot, whistle
Wing Wangs: Chinese sword-sticks
Wun Wong Eye: eye-patch
Wun Wong Arm: hook
Wun Wong Leg: peg-leg
Dora: box of matches, clip-on pencils, filthy rag
Wordsworth: packet of confetti

LIGHTING PLOT

Property fittings required: nil
An open stage

ACT I

To open: House Lights up as **Mr Macaroni** welcomes audience

Cue 1	**All:** "Luigi Macaroni!" *Bring up warm general lighting; fade* *House Lights*	(Page 1)
Cue 2	**Dora** sits in chair *Fade to spot on Dora*	(Page 5)
Cue 3	**Dora:** "That's it!" *Return to previous lighting*	(Page 5)
Cue 4	**Eileen** and **Norman** bring chairs DS *Fade to warm pink lighting concentrated DS*	(Page 10)
Cue 5	As hair-drier "explodes" *Black-out*	(Page 13)
Cue 6	**Eileen:** "Emergency lights quickly." *Return to previous lighting*	(Page 13)
Cue 7	**Wordsworth:** "Let's get in the mood." *Fade lights to Arabian hue*	(Page 16)
Cue 8	**Wordsworth** claps his hands *Return to previous lighting*	(Page 18)

ACT II

Cue 9	When ready *Fade House Lights; bring up blue lighting*	(Page 21)
Cue 10	**Wangs:** "Kung Fu calls." *Change to warm pink lighting*	(Page 21)
Cue 11	**All:** "Bingo!" *Black-out*	(Page 29)
Cue 12	When ready *Return to previous lighting*	(Page 30)

EFFECTS PLOT

To give the desired seaside mood, the sound of seagulls should be heard at times during the play, at the director's discretion.

ACT I

ACT II

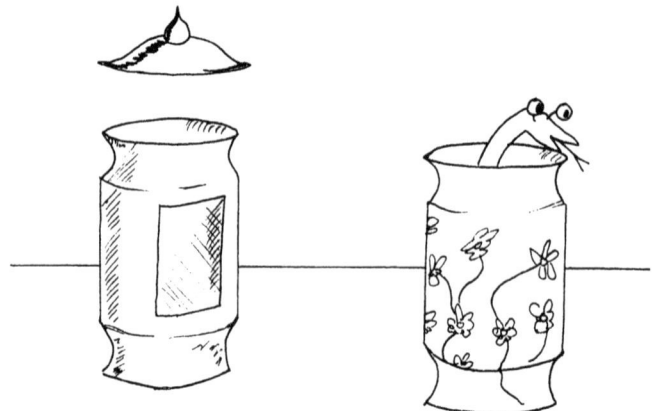

Construction of Snake Jar

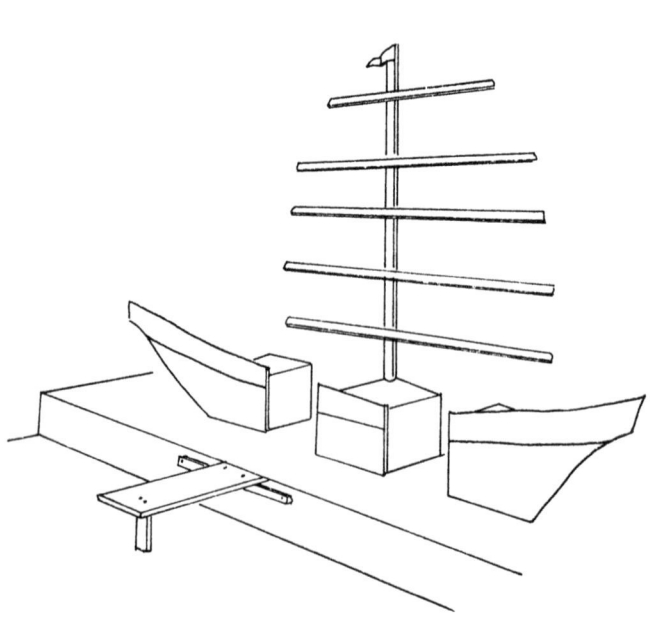

Construction of Chinese Junk

Albert the Snake

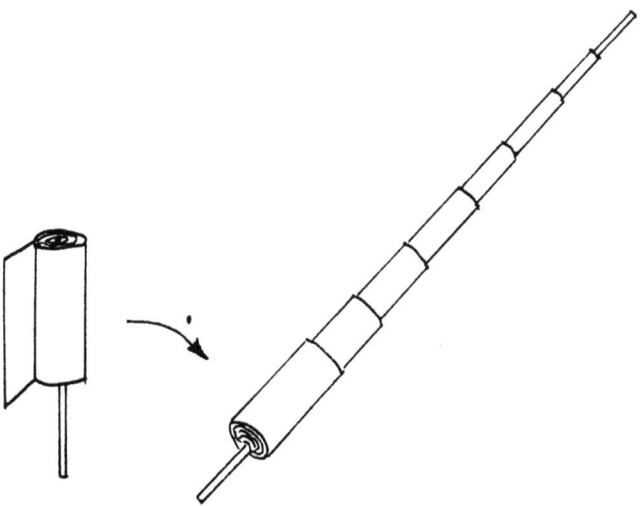

Chinese Sword-sticks

MADE AND PRINTED IN GREAT BRITAIN BY
LATIMER TREND & COMPANY LTD PLYMOUTH
MADE IN ENGLAND

www.ingramcontent.com/pod-product-compliance
Ingram Content Group UK Ltd.
Pitfield, Milton Keynes, MK11 3LW, UK
UKHW020914101225
3797IPUK00019BA/85

9 780573 050626